Introduction & Contents

If you enjoy your parchment craft you will also want to master gridwork - that amazingly intricate kind of lace detail which so often frames parchment art. Traditionally, it is quite complicated, and involves lots of counting and focus !

Tina Cox has come up with a brilliant gridwork solution. She is one of the most creative parchers you could wish to meet. Her work is original, fresh and funky, and she is forever coming up with great designs and ideas. These Groovi Pattern grids, for example. She has developed a whole series of Border Pattern grids - straight and diagonal - and you will be baffled what can be created with a few strategically drilled holes in an acrylic plate. I know I was.

In this clever little ii-book, Tina takes you through basic patterns using just one of the border grids, *Straight Border Pattern Grid No. 1,* one pattern at a time. She explains perforating and embossing, and a combination of the two. She shows you how to create gridwork, not only in a straight line, but also on a curve. There are lovely step-by-step projects with lucid instructions to follow throughout, too.

If you were wanting to get to grips with that wonderful lacey gridwork, then the first Straight Border Pattern grid plus this book wi'' '   es me
that she will write at least another little bool   r grid
once we're ready to take it to the next level ! C

Have fun,
Barbara Gray

3

Tools you'll need

Clarity Lightwave
A4 Translucent Piercing Mat
Groovi Plate Starter Kit
Groovi Border Plate Mate
Groovi Baby Plate Mate
Border Pattern Grid Straight No. 1
A Basic Grid Straight
Groovi Single Needle Perforating Tool or
Pergamano Bold 1-needle tool
Pergamano 1mm ball tool
Pergamano Scissors or Perga Cutter
Groovi Guard
Groovi Sticker Tabs

The Grid

This Border Pattern Grid comprises five basic patterns.

These pattern grids can be used to emboss or perforate.
Emboss from the back and perforate from the front.

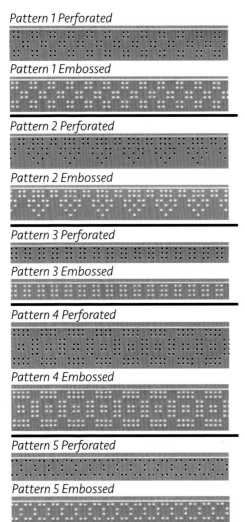

Pattern 1 Perforated

Pattern 1 Embossed

Pattern 2 Perforated

Pattern 2 Embossed

Pattern 3 Perforated

Pattern 3 Embossed

Pattern 4 Perforated

Pattern 4 Embossed

Pattern 5 Perforated

Pattern 5 Embossed

Perforated & Embossed

ALONG A STRAIGHT LINE

Here we see each of the 5 patterns either embossed or perforated along a straight line, just as they come on the pattern grid.

You can also combine embossing and perforating to produce beautiful lacework.

See instructions below and overleaf.

Perforating & Embossing

COMBINED

1. If starting with embossing

a. Attach parchment on pattern grid, back facing up.

b. Emboss pattern with No. 2 ball tool from Starter Kit, or 1mm Pergamano ball tool.

c. Remove from grid.

d. Turn parchment around, line up embossed dots on straight basic grid & attach.

e. Perforate design between embossed dots using 1-needle tool.

2. If starting with perforating

a. Attach parchment on pattern grid, front facing up.

b. Perforate pattern with 1-needle tool.

c. Remove from grid.

d. Turn parchment around, line up perforated holes on straight basic grid and attach.

e. Emboss the design between the perforated holes, again using the No. 2 or the 1mm BT

Perforated & Embossed

AROUND A CIRCLE

Below you will find images and instructions how to perforate and emboss around a circle, using the Groovi® Straight No. 1 Border Pattern Grid. In this example, pattern 2 from the grid has been used. The same instructions will work for some but not all of the other patterns.

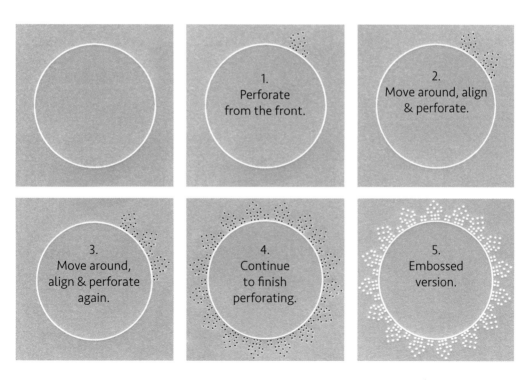

1.
Perforate
from the front.

2.
Move around, align
& perforate.

3.
Move around,
align & perforate
again.

4.
Continue
to finish
perforating.

5.
Embossed
version.

Perforated & Embossed

AROUND A SQUARE

Below you will find images and instructions how to perforate and emboss around a square using the Groovi® Straight No. 1 Border Pattern Grid. In this example, pattern 4 from the grid has been used. The same instructions will work for some but not all of the other patterns.

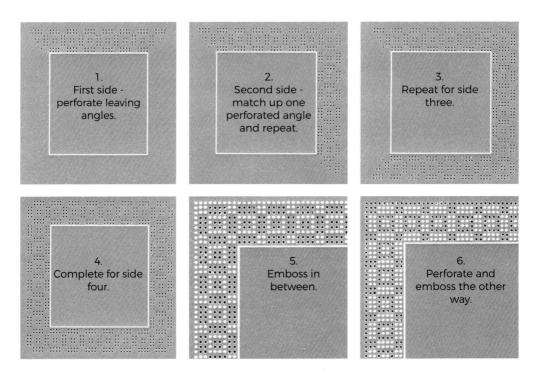

1.
First side - perforate leaving angles.

2.
Second side - match up one perforated angle and repeat.

3.
Repeat for side three.

4.
Complete for side four.

5.
Emboss in between.

6.
Perforate and emboss the other way.

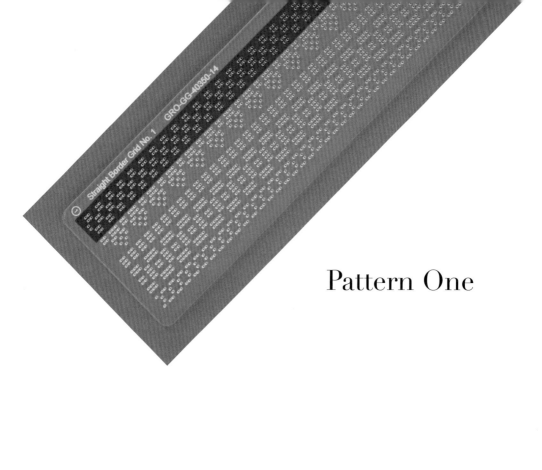

Pattern One

Pattern One, Perforated & Embossed

A QUICK HOW-TO USING PATTERN 1

The following is a guide to perforating and embossing the first pattern on the grid along a straight line. The images and instructions explain how to combine embossing and perforating techniques in order to create patterns that can be used in your parchment craft designs. Pages 8, 9 and 10 contain examples of completed card projects, designed by Tina Cox. Each card is an example of how this first pattern can be used to embellish your parchment art. These quick how-to guides, and example projects are repeated throughout the book for each of the five patterns on the grid.

Example 1

1. Using pattern 1, emboss one row.

2. Turn to front & perforate in between.

3. Perforate top line on basic grid straight.

4. Or emboss.

Example 2

1. Perforate two rows.

2. Turn around and emboss between first row.

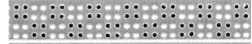

3. Emboss between second row.

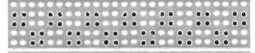

4. Emboss above top row on basic grid straight.

Example 3

1. Emboss all three rows.

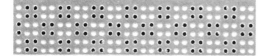

2. Turn around and perforate between all of the embossed rows.

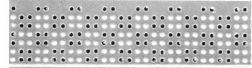

3. Perforate above top row of embossed dots on basic grid straight.

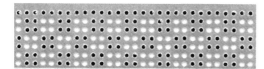

4. OR, perforate every hole above the top row on basic grid straight.

Example 4

1. Perforate all three rows.

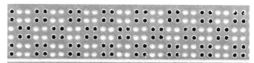

2. Turn around and emboss between all of the perforated rows.

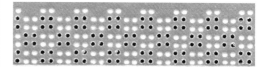

3. Emboss above top row of perforated dots on basic grid straight.

4. OR, Emboss every hole above the top row on basic grid straight.

11

Framed Florals Birthday Card

DESIGNED USING PATTERN 1

Ingredients

Groovi Grids: *Straight Border Pattern Grid No.1, and Basic Grid Straight.*
Groovi Border Plates: *Henna Border, and Best Wishes Sentiments.* **Groovi A5 Square Plates:** *Sprig Background, Meadow Grasses, and Nested Squares.*

To Make

1. Emboss a square on regular parchment paper.

2. Emboss and perforate one row of the design from Pattern 1 inside the square.

3. Emboss 2 rectangles, one with a double outline and the other larger one behind it.

4. Emboss the flower, trellis, scallop border and greetings in place.

5. Add colour on the back of the design using Distress Markers.

6. Emboss and perforate one row of the design from Pattern 1 inside the double outlined rectangle.

7. Cut the piece to size just outside the square. Using brads, mount onto a piece of pink parchment and white card with the same dimensions. Attach this whole piece onto a folded white card.

Birthday Candles

DESIGNED USING PATTERN 1

Ingredients

Groovi Grids: *Straight Border Pattern Grid No.1, Basic Grid Straight, and Basic Grid Diagonal.* **Groovi Baby Plates:** *Art Deco Lady.* **Groovi Border Plates:** *Henna Border, and Best Wishes Sentiments.* **Groovi A5 Square Plates:** *Nested Squares, Universal Framer.* **Groovi A4 Square Plates:** *Alphabet Picture Frame.* **Groovi Templates:** *Cake Box Template.*

To Make

1. Emboss a square on blue parchment paper.

2. Inside the square, emboss the design using the various plates. Colour with the Gold Sakura pen on the front. Colour the confetti and candles with Distress Markers on the back.

3. Emboss and perforate one row of the design from Pattern 1 inside the double outlined square.

4. Emboss dots between the square and frame using the Basic Grid Diagonal and cut just outside the square.

5. On regular parchment paper, emboss a square and create the perforated/embossed border on the inside. Cut to size.

6. Using brads, mount the blue parchment piece on the regular parchment piece and blue card. Attach this whole piece onto a folded white card.

Christmas Baubles

DESIGNED USING PATTERN 1

Ingredients

Groovi Grids: *Straight Border Pattern Grid No.1, and Basic Grid Straight.*
Groovi Border Plates: *Christmas Baubles.* **Groovi A5 Square Plates:**
Nested Squares.

To Make

1. Emboss a square on pink parchment paper.

2. Emboss one row of the design from Pattern 1 to create boxes inside the square.

3. Inside the patterned squares, emboss the design using the various plates.

4. On regular parchment paper, create the perforated/embossed border from Pattern 1 and on the Basic Grid Straight emboss dots on the inside and outside of the patterned border. Cut to size.

5. Using brads, mount the pink parchment piece on the regular parchment piece and pink card. Attach this whole piece onto a folded white card.

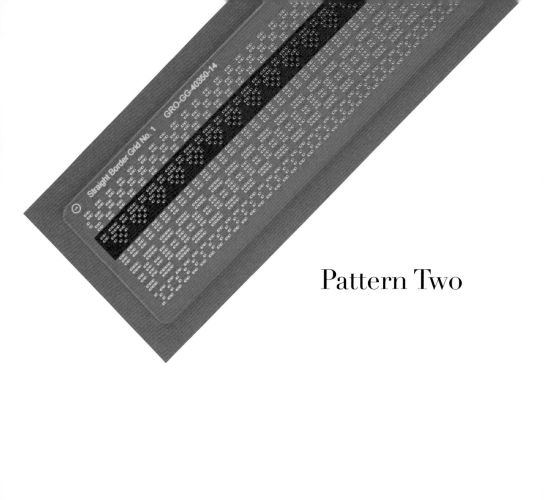

Pattern Two

Pattern Two, Perforated & Embossed

Example 1

1. Emboss pattern.

2. Turn around and perforate in between on a Basic Grid Straight

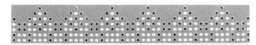

3. Perforate outside of the embossed on a Basic Grid Straight

Example 2

1. Perforate pattern.

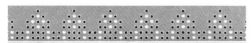

2. Turn around and emboss in between perforations on a Basic Grid Straight.

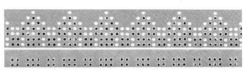

3. Emboss outside the perforated pattern on a Basic Grid Straight.

Example 3

1. Perforate bottom row.

2. Turn around and emboss hearts.

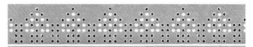

3. Turn around and perforate between embossing on a Basic Grid Straight.

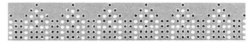

4. Turn around and emboss remaining holes on a Basic Grid Straight.

19

Floral Braids

Ingredients

Groovi Grids: *Straight Border Pattern Grid No.1.* **Groovi Baby Plates:** *Amaryllis Cameo.* **Groovi Border Plates:** *Cake Decorations.* **Groovi A5 Square Plates:** *Nested Squares.*

To Make

1. Emboss 2 squares on regular parchment paper.

2. Emboss the design from Pattern 2 inside the double outlined square.

3. Emboss the rest of the design inside and outside the squares.

4. Colour on the back using bendable pencils. Cut out around the outside of the frilly edge.

5. Using brads, mat and layer the parchment piece onto a light blue parchment piece, white card and dark blue parchment. Attach this whole piece onto a folded white card.

Flowery Swirls

DESIGNED USING PATTERN 2

Ingredients

Groovi Grids: *Straight Border Pattern Grid No.1, and Basic Grid Straight.*
Groovi Border Plates: *Cake Decorations, and Floral Border.* **Groovi A5 Square Plates:** *Nested Squares.*

To Make

1. Emboss 2 squares on regular parchment paper.

2. Emboss/perforate the design from Pattern 2 inside the double outlined square and cut outside and inside the outlines to create a frame.

3. On blue parchment paper emboss the same size square as above and along the outside square, emboss the design from Pattern 2.

4. Emboss a row of dots and corners using the Basic Grid Straight Straight.

5. Emboss more squares outside and inside the gridded borders and the rest of the designs.

6. Colour on the back using Distress Markers and cut to size.

7. Using brads mount the regular parchment frame onto the blue parchment, regular parchment and blue card. Attach this whole piece onto a folded white card.

Love To You

Ingredients

Groovi Grids: *Straight Border Pattern Grid No.1.* **Groovi Border Plates:** *Occasions.* **Groovi A5 Square Plates:** *Nested Squares, Nested Circles, Music Notes, Roses 1, and Roses 2.*

To Make

1. Emboss a square and 3 circles inside the square on regular parchment paper.

2. Emboss/perforate the design from pattern 2 around the smallest circle.

3. On the Basic Grid Straight, emboss dots in the bigger double outlined circles.

4. Emboss the rest of the design inside the circles and on the corners of the square outlines.

5. Colour on the back using Distress Markers and cut to size.

6. Using brads mount the piece onto pink parchment and white card which has been cut slightly larger. Attach this whole piece onto folded white card.

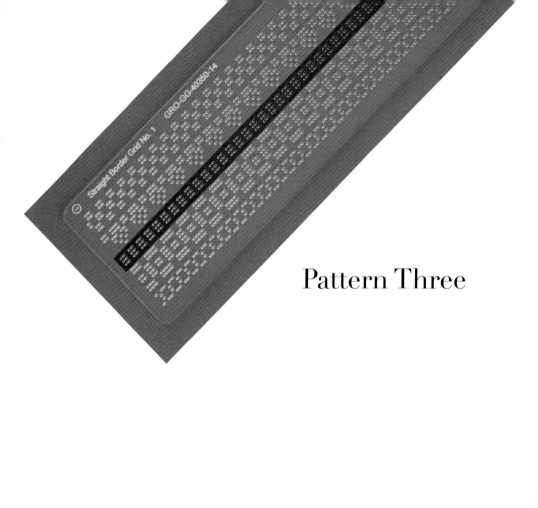

Pattern Three

Pattern Three, Perforated & Embossed

A QUICK HOW-TO USING PATTERN 3

Example 1

1. Emboss row.

2. Turn around & perforate between embossed dots on Basic Grid Straight

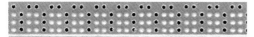

3. Perforate holes above the embossed dots on Basic Grid Straight.

Example 2

1. Perforate row.

2. Turn around & emboss between perforations on Basic Grid Straight

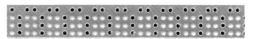

3. Emboss a whole row dots above the pattern on Basic Grid Straight

Example 3

1. Emboss top and bottom dots of pattern.

2. Turn around and perforate middle dots.

3. Perforate between the top and bottom dots on Basic Grid Straight

4. Turn around and emboss between the middle perforated holes on Basic Grid Straight

Just Dream

Ingredients

Groovi Grids: *Straight Border Pattern Grid No.1, and Basic Grid Straight.*
Groovi Baby Plates: *Art Deco Lady.* **Groovi Border Plates:** *Floral Squares - Daisy.* **Groovi A5 Square Plates:** *Nested Squares, Large Lace Netting, and Sprig Background.* **Groovi A4 Square Plates:** *Alphabet Picture Frame.*

To Make

1. On pink parchment, emboss the square and design inside. Colour flowers on the front with Sakura gold pen and the rest on the back with Distress Markers. Cut to size.

2. on regular parchment, emboss 3 squares and perforate the design from Pattern 3 in the inner square and in the outer square, emboss the design from Pattern 3. Cut to size.

3. Emboss/perforate the design from Pattern 3 on pink parchment and emboss a row of dots around the edge using the Basic Straight Grid. Cut to size.

4. Mount the flower pink piece onto the regular and pink gridded pieces and pink card. Attach the whole piece onto folded white card.

Peace & Hope

Ingredients

Groovi Grids: *Straight Border Pattern Grid No.1, and Basic Grid Straight.* **Groovi Baby Plates:** *Wren & Vine.* **Groovi A5 Square Plates:** *Nested Squares, Dove Window, and Madonna Window.* **Groovi Plate Mate:** *Border Plate Mate.*

To Make

1. On blue parchment, emboss a double outline square.

2. Emboss the design inside the square and colour on the back using Distress Markers.

3. Emboss/perforate the design from Pattern 3 inside the double outlined square. Cut to size.

4. On regular parchment, emboss a double square and the greeting and design inside the square. Colour on the back with Distress Markers.

5. Emboss/perforate the design from Pattern 3 inside the double outlined square. Cut to size.

6. Using brads mount the blue parchment piece onto the regular parchment piece, blue parchment piece and white card which has been cut to size. Attach this whole piece onto a folded white card.

Best Wishes

Fuchsia Butterfly

Ingredients

Groovi Grids: *Straight Border Pattern Grid No.1, and Basic Grid Straight.*
Groovi Border Plates: *Occasions.* **Groovi A5 Square Plates:** *Nested Squares, Nested Circles, Jayne's Fuchsias, Jayne's Dahlias - Name, and Woven.*

To Make

1. Emboss a circle on regular parchment paper. Emboss the design inside. Colour on the back with Distress Markers and cut to size.

2. On regular parchment paper, emboss a double outlined square and the design and greeting inside. Colour on the back.

3. Emboss/perforate the design from Pattern 3 within the double outlined square and inside the rectangles of the woven border. Cut to size.

4. Mount the round parchment piece onto to a pink card circle. Then mount onto the square parchment piece, pink parchment, white card and pink card using brads. Attach this whole piece onto a folded white card.

5. Create a 3D butterfly from regular parchment paper, colour it and attach on the right side of the card above the fuchsia with Perga Glue.

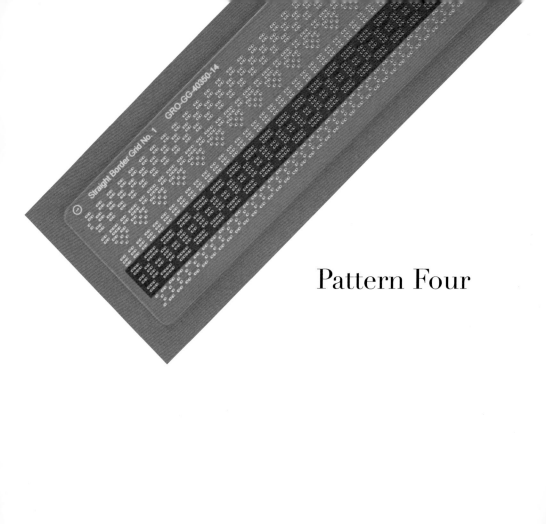

Pattern Four

Pattern Four, Perforated & Embossed

A QUICK HOW-TO USING PATTERN 4

Example 1

1. Emboss pattern.

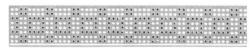

2. Turn around and perforate between all embossing on Basic Grid Straight.

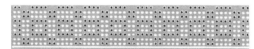

3. Perforate above top embossed row on Basic Grid Straight.

Example 2

1. Perforate pattern.

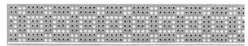

2. Turn around and emboss between all perforations on Basic Grid Straight.

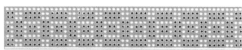

3. Emboss every hole above top row on Basic Grid Straight

Example 3

1. Perforate top and bottom row.

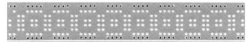

2. Turn around and emboss in between pattern.

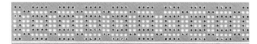

3. Turn around and perforate between embossed dots on Basic Grid Straight.

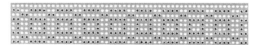

4. Turn around and emboss in between and above top row on Basic Grid Straight.

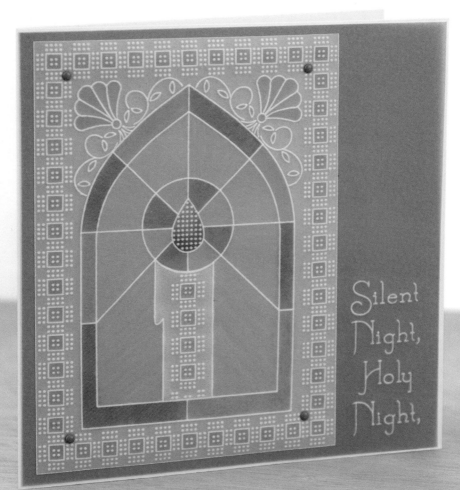

Silent
Night,

Holy
Night,

Silent Night, Holy Night

DESIGNED USING PATTERN 4

Ingredients

Groovi Grids: *Straight Border Pattern Grid No.1, and Basic Grid Straight.*
Groovi Baby Plates: *Square Nested.* **Groovi Border Plates:** *Lace Corners.*
Groovi A5 Square Plates: *Silent Night.*

To Make

1. Emboss a rectangle on regular parchment paper. Emboss the design from Pattern 4 inside the rectangle. Emboss the rest of the design inside this piece.

2. Inside the candle, emboss the design from Pattern 4.

3. In the candle flame emboss the dots from the Basic Grid Straight.

4. Colour on the back using Distress Markers. Cut to size.

5. On pink parchment, emboss the words and cut to size.

6. Using brads, mount the regular parchment piece onto the pink parchment piece and a piece of white card cut to size. Attach this whole piece onto a folded white card.

Just To Say

Just To Say

Ingredients

Groovi Grids: *Straight Border Pattern Grid No.1, and Basic Grid Straight .*
Groovi A5 Square Plates: *Mountains & Hills, Bamboo, and Universal Framer.*

To Make

1. On regular parchment, emboss a double outline square.

2. Emboss the design and greeting inside the square and emboss random dots on the leaves from the Basic Grid Straight. Colour on the back with Distress Markers.

3. Emboss the design from Pattern 4 inside the double outlined square. Cut to size.

4. Using brads mount this piece on to a pink parchment piece and white card cut to a slightly larger size.

5. On pink parchment, emboss/perforate a strip of the design from Pattern 4 that is long enough to fold around the square piece.

6. Place this strip in position, fold around and stick on the back of the above mounted piece. Attach this whole piece onto a folded white card.

7. To create the butterfly, emboss the outside outlines of the butterfly on pink parchment and the rest of the butterfly on regular parchment. Colour the butterfly on the back. Cut out, layer and attach to the card.

Agapanthus On Blue

DESIGNED USING PATTERN 4

Ingredients

Groovi Grids: *Straight Border Pattern Grid No.1, and Basic Grid Straight.*
Groovi Border Plates: *Cake Decorations.* **Groovi A5 Square Plates:** *Nested Squares, Agapanthus, and Roses.*

To Make

1. Emboss a square on blue parchment paper. Inside the square emboss a panel on the bottom.

2. Emboss the scallop edges on the top and bottom of the panel followed by the flower bouquet and colour on the back with Distress Markers.

3. In the panel and top corners of the square, emboss/perforate the design from Pattern 4 and cut the square to size.

4. Using the corner punch, mount this piece onto blue card and attach onto a folded white card.

5. Emboss, colour and cut the butterfly on regular parchment paper and attach.

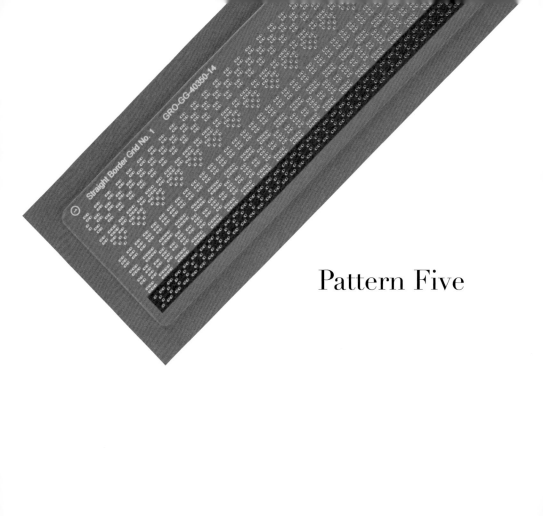

Straight Border Grid No. 1   GRO-GG-40350-14

Pattern Five

Pattern Five, Perforated & Embossed

A QUICK HOW-TO USING PATTERN 5

Example 1

1. Emboss pattern.

2. Turn around and perforate in between on Basic Grid Straight.

3. Perforate every hole above the pattern on Basic Grid Straight.

Example 2

1. Perforate pattern.

2. Turn around and emboss in between on Basic Grid Straight.

3. Emboss above the top row of the perforations on Basic Grid Straight.

Example 3

1. Perforate pattern.

2. Emboss between every other perforated pattern and between top and bottom perforated holes. Also emboss above the top row of perforated holes on Basic Grid Straight.

3. Perforate between the patterns that still remain empty and above the top embossed row on Basic Grid Straight.

Ornamental Vase

Ingredients

Groovi Grids: *Straight Border Pattern Grid No.1, and Basic Grid Straight.*
Groovi Baby Plates: *Vases.* **Groovi A5 Square Plates:** *Nested Squares, Art Nouveau Poppies, and Texture.*

To Make

1. On regular parchment paper, emboss square and the design inside. Colour the design from the back with Distress Markers.

2. On the bottom, create a border of 2 rows of the design from Pattern 5 by embossing and perforating. Cut on three sides and tear on the right side.

3. On blue parchment, emboss a double square outline. Emboss the design inside and colour.

4. By holding the regular parchment piece on this piece, mark where to put the border design so that it lines up. Emboss and perforate the design from Pattern 5. Cut to size.

5. Using brads mount the poppy piece onto the blue parchment piece and another blue parchment square. Wrap a ribbon in between the 2 borders and tie into a bow. Use double-sided adhesive to fasten at the back. Attach this piece onto a white folded card.

Pretty Border Butterfly

Ingredients

Groovi Grids: *Straight Border Pattern Grid No.1, and Basic Grid Straight.*
Groovi Border Plates: *Cake Decorations.* **Groovi A5 Square Plates:**
Nested Squares, Jayne's Butterflies, and Universal Framer.

To Make

1. Emboss 3 squares on pink parchment.

2. Inside the square, emboss a butterfly. On the outside of the innermost square, emboss the fan border design. Colour on the back with Distress Markers.

3. Emboss/perforate the design from Pattern 5 within the outside double square. Also emboss a border on the left and right of the butterfly and in the corners.

4. Emboss the greeting under the horizontal border design at the centre of the card..

5. Cut the piece to size. Using brads, mount this onto darker pink parchment and pink card. Attach this whole piece onto a folded white card.

A Friendly Pheasant

DESIGNED USING PATTERN 5

Ingredients

Groovi Grids: *Straight Border Pattern Grid No.1, Basic Grid Straight, and Basic Grid Diagonal .* **Groovi Baby Plates:** *Wren & Daisies, and Funky Birds.* **Groovi Border Plates:** *Lace 1.* **Groovi Border Plates:** *Lace 1.* **Groovi A5 Square Plates:** *Nested Squares, Nested Circles, Waterhouse, and Leafy Swirl.*

To Make

1. On blue parchment paper, emboss a double outline circle. Now emboss a double outline square, with the embossed circle in the bottom right hand corner. Emboss the rest of the design inside the square and circle.

2. Within the leaves, emboss dots from the Basic Grid Diagonal. Colour the design from the back using Distress Markers.

3. Outside the square, emboss/perforate the design from Pattern 5. Add a row of dots outside the border from the Basic Grid Straight. Cut to size.

4. Using brads, mount this piece onto blue card and then attach it onto a folded white card.

The Big Project

Ingredients

Groovi Grids: *Straight Border Pattern Grid No.1, Basic Grid Straight,*
Groovi Starter Kit.
Groovi A5 Square Plates: *Nested Squares, Nested Circles, Sprig plate*

Now let's put our knowledge to the test and our new skills into practice.

The following is a step-by-step guide using the Straight No.1 Pattern Grid, the Groovi® Starter Kit, the nested square and circle plates, and the A5 Sprig Background plate.

1. Emboss a tree and a double outline circle.

2. Emboss the leaves from the Sprig plate at the top.

3. Emboss sun, landscape and birds.
   (*Birds made using brackets from A5 square plate mate*).

4. Emboss square outside circle, and use the same nested square plate to introduce the chequer lines.

5. Emboss outside squares leaving 1 square space in between.
Emboss dots between double circle outlines using Basis grid Straight.

6. Perforate grid patterns on front in corner. Turn around and emboss in between. Emboss outside holes.

a) Perforate patterns on front.

b) Turn around and emboss in between.

c) Emboss outside perforated border.

d) Emboss semi-circles between the embossed/perforated border.

7. a / b / c / d are written around the diagram.

8. Emboss Pattern 3 on back. Turn to front and perforate between embossed dots. Perforate in corners.

Colouring & Finishing

Colour in on the back using a selection of Distress Markers.
Using brads, layer up the piece onto blue parchment and white card
the same size as the blue parchment.
Attach this whole piece on folded white card to finish.